Tulip Mania: The History and Legacy of the ...ative Bubble during the Dutch Go...

By Charles River Editors

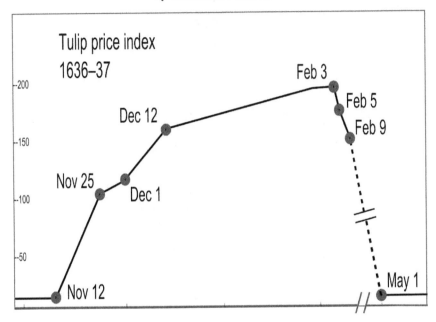

Jay Henry's graph of the tulip price's dramatic rise and fall in the Netherlands

About Charles River Editors

Charles River Editors is a boutique digital publishing company, specializing in bringing history back to life with educational and engaging books on a wide range of topics. Keep up to date with our new and free offerings with this 5 second sign up on our weekly mailing list, and visit Our Kindle Author Page to see other recently published Kindle titles.

We make these books for you and always want to know our readers' opinions, so we encourage you to leave reviews and look forward to publishing new and exciting titles each week.

Introduction

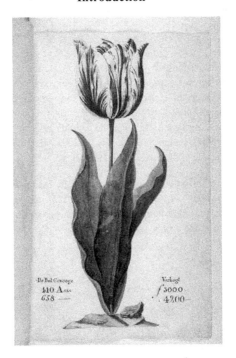

**A tulip, known as "the Viceroy" (viseroij), displayed in the 1637 Dutch catalog
Verzameling van een Meenigte Tulipaanen**

Tulip Mania

If one were to glide over the Dutch countryside via helicopter in the springtime, the beauty below them would seem almost surreal. The rolling rectangular fields are composed of immaculately neat, horizontal stripes in vibrant swatches of scarlet, pink, lavender, cream-white, and midnight-blue. The ethereal sight is even more breathtaking when one takes a stroll along these fields, surrounded by endless carpets of bright color. These world-famous three-petal, three-sepal flowers, all craning their necks towards the dazzling sun, are none other than Dutch tulips.

The Netherlands is now the world's leading commercial producer of tulips, shipping out more than 3 billion of these colorful beauties each year. Standard tulips, depending on where one is based, typically sell for anywhere between $1.00 to $3.50 USD per stem today. They are a creative alternative to roses, lilies, and other traditional flowers. Needless to say, like every other floral breed, special tulips – such as hybrids, or ones with unique, multi-colored streaks and patterns – will cost buyers a pretty penny, but a bouquet is certainly not going to break the bank.

Legend has it, however, that this was not always the case. As a matter of fact, these delightful "harbingers of spring" were supposedly once so rabidly sought-after that it wasn't just more valuable than gold – men threw themselves into financial ruin all for the sake of attaining just one of these sacred flowers. At the crescendo of what is now remembered as "Tulip Mania," or the "Tulip Craze," a single, shallot-like bulb of an unripe tulip was worth 20 times the annual salary of a skilled laborer. This aggressively volatile period, marked by convoluted and careless market speculation, inevitably culminated in the disastrous bursting of one of the world's first financial bubbles, an example of the perils of herd mentality.

But how much truth is there to this oft-repeated story of the *Tulpenmanie,* really? *Tulip Mania: The History and Legacy of the World's First Speculative Bubble during the Dutch Golden Age* analyzes the legendary mania, and whether it was as dramatic as portrayed. Along with pictures of important people, places, and events, you will learn about Tulip Mania like never before.

.

Budding Prospects

"Something about the way they twist

As if to catch the last applause,

And drink the moment through long straws,

And how, tomorrow, they'll be missed..." - A. E. Stallings, "Tulips" (2009)

The infamous tulip bubble and the aftermath following the prod of the needle is now a golden lesson for what to avoid in business. In the 2010 film *Wall Street 2: Money Never Sleeps*, Gordon Gekko keeps a framed memorial of the tulip upset in his office. "Bubbles, they crash. Like these tulips. This is the greatest bubble story of all time. Back in the 1600s, the Dutch, they get speculation fever to the point that you could buy a beautiful house on a canal in Amsterdam for the price of one bulb. They called it 'Tulip Mania.' Then it collapsed – you could buy 10 tulips for $2. People got wiped out, but you know, who remembers?"

This riveting tale, packed with mob mentality, surprising violence, and lightning-paced developments, is indeed one that folks from all walks of life can certainly learn from, but how much truth is there to this oft-repeated financial parable? To better answer this question, one must first examine how and why exactly these tulips were so prized in the first place.

Like most things that people hold dear to their heart, tulips were not native to Europe, but rather the faraway lands in Central Asia, which immediately validated the flower as an exotic import available only to the upper echelons of society. The very first batches of wild tulips are believed to have first sprouted along the steppes of Armenia, Persia, and the Caucasus regions, before naturally spreading to the fields along the fringes of China, the Hindu Kush, and Turkish Kazakhstan in the 1st millennium CE. As evidenced by the tulips that appear in 12th century motifs produced by the Seljuks in Konya, the flowers eventually penetrated Anatolian soil from the Turkish lands.

Other chroniclers suggest that the tulip owes its prestige to an age-old story straight out of Turkish lore. There was once a dashing Prince Farhad (also identified as a sculptor in other accounts) who fell head over heels for a gorgeous palace maid named Shirin. When the disconsolate Shirin slit her own neck to avoid marrying the repulsive King Khosrow, the heartbroken Farhad mounted his stallion and deliberately charged off a cliff, plunging to his death. The pool of blood that trickled out of Farhad's cracked skull and shattered limbs seeped into the earth. For every drop of crimson, a blood-red tulip sprung up from the earth, thereby "making the flower a historic symbol of 'perfect love'."

In fact, long before tulips arose as a status symbol in the Dutch community, the tulip was already a fixture of its own in the mystical spheres of Anatolian culture. A *Sufi* (local mystic) by the name of Rumi, for instance, frequently peppered tulips into his poems. One such poem, entitled "So Recklessly Exposed," reads as follows:

"December and January, gone.

Tulips coming up.

It's time to watch how trees stagger in the wind

And roses never rest..."

Islamic creative spirits were also particularly fond of the tulip, which many say is due to the flower's resemblance to the Arabic word that translates into "Allah." As such, ornamental tiles in countless mosques, as well as a multitude of textiles sported by the masses, featured these hallowed flowers.

Sultan Mehmed II, known as Mehmed the Conqueror, was a 15th century ruler of the Ottoman Empire and among the first prominent figures to fall in love with these elegant, brightly-colored flowers. Gifted with a green thumb himself, the sultan stunned both intruders and defenders alike by planting swathes of tulips, carnations, roses, and other fragrant fruit trees around the city walls.

Mehmed II

Sultan Suleiman the Magnificent, who inherited the empire in 1520, was even more smitten with these rainbow blossoms. It was during his reign that tulip farming was transformed into a legitimate profession for the first time in Istanbul, and by the end of his rule, local farmers were planting more tulips than they were roses and other classic flowers. The sultan, a prolific wordsmith who published poems under the name "Muhibbi," also paid numerous tributes to the beloved flower in his work.

Suleiman the Magnificent

Perhaps not surprisingly, Suleiman's love for tulips was infectious, and in short order his subjects also became bewitched by these brilliant blossoms, some to the point of dangerous obsession. Several accounts tell of an unnamed sultan who went on such a frenzied spending spree at a tulip festival that he bankrupted the royal treasury, an unforgivable crime that ultimately cost him his head. In a nutshell, an extreme fascination with tulips was anything but a new phenomenon.

How exactly the first tulips made it to northwest Europe is still widely contested. Some say it was Lopo Vaz de Sampayo, governor of Portuguese India between 1526 and 1529, who smuggled the first tulips to Portugal from Sri Lanka following an unceremonious tumble from grace. Unfortunately, the story is punctured with several holes, the most glaring of them being the fact that tulips did not grow naturally in Sri Lanka.

Today, most historians assume that it was Oghier Ghislain de Busbecq, Holy Roman Emperor Ferdinand I's ambassador to the Ottoman Empire between 1555 and 1562, who introduced the tulips into European culture. Busbecq first chanced upon these lovely flowers upon one of his first visits to Constantinople, where he was tasked with negotiating a border treaty regarding the territory of Transylvania. His journal entries reveal his captivation with Suleiman's gardens, which were overflowing with "an abundance of flowers everywhere; narcissus, hyacinths, and those which in Turkish Lale, much to our astonishment, because it was almost midwinter, a season unfriendly to flowers."

Oghier Ghislain de Busbecq

Ferdinand I

   Come April of 1559, Swiss naturalist Conrad Gessner reportedly witnessed the first successful batch of ruby-red tulips in the garden of Councilor Johann Heinrich Herwart, an Augsburg magistrate. This species was later christened the *"tulipa turcarum,"* which would mean that a parcel of tulip bulbs was sent to Bavaria – perhaps courtesy of Busbecq – sometime in early 1555 and planted in autumn of that same year so as to withstand the frost of winter. In 1561, Gessner's colored sketch of the red tulip was published as a woodblock print for the first time in a compilation entitled *"De Hortis Germaniae Liber Recens."* More of these delicate tulip woodcuts were published in the decades that followed.

   It was during this time that a Latinized name for the flower was coined. Tulips were originally referred to as *"tülbend,"* the Turkish term for "turban," because the silhouette of a tulip was reminiscent of a sultan's bulbous turban. It may also have been inspired by the Persian word *"dulband,"* or "round." The Flemish, Dutch, and other Europeans dubbed the flower *"tulipan,"* and it was eventually shortened to "tulip" when the bulbs later made it to English soil.

The tulip's debut in the Netherlands, while just as hazy, is most frequently attributed to Flemish botanist Charles de l'Écluse (also spelled "Carolus Clusius"). In 1572, Clusius, then stationed in Prague, received a handful of precious Turkish tulip bulbs from Busbecq, one of his dearest friends. Freshly appointed as the prefect of Holy Roman Emperor Maximilian II's imperial herb/medical garden in Vienna, Clusius eagerly experimented with these whimsical bulbs. Whether or not he managed to successfully harvest any tulips from Maximilian's garden is unclear, but either way, when Rudolf II rose to power in 1576, the new sovereign stripped the garden bare and built in its stead a training ground for equestrians.

Clusius

Now that his services were no longer needed, Clusius carefully pocketed what was left of his bulbs and relocated to Frankfurt in 1577. There, he acquired a humble plot of land and continued to tend his plants for the next 16 years. In autumn of 1590, either prompted by religious persecution or simply a promising job offer, 64-year-old Clusius agreed to uproot once again to Leiden in the Netherlands, where, as the honorary professor of botany for the University of Leiden, he would design and preside over the new medicinal *hortus academicus* (academic garden).

By the time Clusius accepted his new post, he had been already been working with tulips (mostly cross-breeding), potatoes, chestnuts, and other foreign plants for several years. Thus, it was in his new garden that he triumphantly planted his tulips for the first time, and by the spring of 1594, the tulips were in full bloom. This day is considered by many of the Dutch as the historic birth of an unlikely flower business that would soon take the region by storm.

Clusius himself ascribed the arrival of tulips in Europe to someone else entirely. French traveler, naturalist, and diplomat Pierre Belon, Clusius asserted, was possibly the first to paint a literary picture of the tulips he spotted in the Levant, referring to them as *"lils rouges"* in his 1553 publication *Les Observations de Plusieurs Singularites*. These divine, unscented lilies he described were most likely tulips since lilies were sparse in Turkey, yet Belon claimed to have seen bountiful patches in every garden.

A few years later, in the 1560s, a Belgian merchant passing through the Levant stumbled across and purchased a few tulip bulbs, which he kept bundled up in a thick square of cloth. Once he returned to Antwerp, the merchant, under the impression that he had picked up onions, roasted two bulbs for supper. Unsurprisingly, the tulip bulbs did not sit well on his taste buds, which led him to discard the rest of the untouched bulbs in his garden. Weeks later, another merchant, Joris Rye from nearby Mechelen, caught sight of the strange bulbs strewn about in the garden. He then scaled the fence and salvaged what he could, successfully breeding the tulips in Mechelen the following spring. Clusius was later quoted as saying, "It is [only] due to [Rye's] care and zeal that I could later see their flowers."

Clusius was thrilled to have been given such an opportunity at the University of Leiden, but the fragile state of his aging body – specifically, his bad hip – prevented him from the daily physical labor required in the garden, his favorite part of the job. He hoped his sore hip would heal by the time the tulips bloomed in the spring of 1594, but when his condition worsened, he had no choice but to employ an extra hand. This assistance came in the form of an apothecary named Dirck Outgaertsz Cluyt from Delft, a city in South Holland. Clusius' mobility eventually improved, but Cluyt remained the director of the *hortus academicus* while his employer held on to his nominal role. Instead, Clusius spent most of his time in his own garden, nurturing his own treasured tulips and greens.

Clusius' rise to prominence in the Dutch field of horticulture coincided with the newfound and rapidly growing interest in botany, partially fueled by the strides made in New World exploration. Gardening and plant cultivation became a hobby associated with the royals, intellectuals, and exclusive upper classes. The upsurge in horticultural encyclopedias, illustrated botanical books, and woodcuts also helped to kindle public interest in the field. The study of plants and cultivation was comfortably established as a credible science, for like Clusius, the bulk of leading botanists at the time held medical degrees, allowing for the discovery of vital medicinal properties in these foreign plants.

Whether or not he had intended to, many say Clusius' very own scientific and literary publications fanned the spreading flames of the public's attraction to the tulip. On top of capturing the breed's unique beauty, one of his books, *Exoticorum libri* (published at the University two years prior to the tulips' first bloom on Dutch soil), noted the tulip's resilience against the tough weather conditions in the Low Countries. A passage from the book reads, "Now, in my old age, when due to my bodily weakness I can scarcely walk, so as not to pass my life completely at leisure, I have applied my mind to the observation of those exotic plants and other things that are brought from foreign parts. Now I have taken on the task of writing the history of all the exotic things that I have acquired in recent years, and that through great efforts I have been able to obtain. I hope that this history, which I have written with great faith and the greatest diligence, will stimulate young men to take up this study in the same way that my earlier observations led them to study of other plants..."

Some were inspired by Clusius' passion for plants and followed in his footsteps, leading to the discovery of a slew of plants previously unheard of, but much to Clusius' disappointment, the better part of his readers had become intrigued by the graceful flower he often praised in his books. The electrifying colors of their petals, which came with a certain air of regality, made these flowers all the more enthralling to the public, and they would quickly become a coveted token of dispensable wealth.

Clusius' discretion about the flowers further whetted the public's appetite, and what many took as Clusius' arrogance did nothing to help his case. Later that year, Clusius expressed his exasperation with the tulip suddenly being thrust into the spotlight. In an indignant letter to a colleague, he groused about what he deemed the overcrowding within the emerging flower industry. Tulips were no longer priceless treasures exchanged amongst genuine collectors; rather, they were now being sold and purchased on the flower market like any other ordinary commodity. Thus, it was Clusius' personal philosophy to turn away anyone that he suspected harbored an ulterior motive, namely selling the bulbs or tulips for a profit. Bearing this in mind, it did not take long for the public to take matters into their own hands. Between the years of 1580 and 1584, and then again in 1596 and 1598, Clusius' garden became the target of a string of midnight thefts, a number of them committed by his very own gardeners and hired help. One time, Clusius returned home from a business trip to find that a dozen of his best bulbs had gone missing, and he later found tulips rising from the ground in his neighbor's garden. The neighbor, a noblewoman, later admitted that she had purchased the tulips from one of Clusius' most trusted servants. None of these incidents, however, broke his heart quite like the morning he awoke to the broken door of his shed, only to find that every last one of the 100 or so bulbs he stashed there were long gone.

Still, there was a silver lining to all of this, as several of the bulbs became displaced and were randomly scattered across the Dutch countryside, allowing for the growth of the Netherlands' first wild tulips. By the 1620s, wild tulips, descended from Clusius' pilfered bulbs, had increased five-fold and had spread to neighboring regions, such as the rural fringes of Alkmaar, Rotterdam, Gouda, Utrecht, and Hoorn.

The Dutch Golden Age

"Take care of the pennies, and the pounds will look after themselves." –Dutch proverb

To many historians, the tulip hysteria that would soon erupt would never have reached such magnitude if it had not been for the concurrent progression of the Dutch Golden Age, which was chugging along at full steam. This gilded era, which lasted roughtly from 1600-1750, catapulted the local economy and culture to new heights. General Manger of Amsterdam's *Rembrandtshuis,* Lidewij de Koekkoek, explained, "The key elements in the Golden Age certainly were creativity, entrepreneurship, an international outlook. The Dutch have always looked outward."

Plainly put, this meant that the Dutch, crowned the masters of the sea and global markets, now had more money to spare. The financial freedom experienced by more and more of the newly-established merchant bourgeoisie allowed even "commoners" to compete in arenas previously sealed off to them. Better yet, the launch of innovative financial institutions, such as "public companies" (firms jointly owned by multiple stock-holding members of the public), meant that even average merchants and businessmen could now swim alongside one another in the profits of mammoth corporations, like the Dutch East India Company (VOC), and later, the Dutch West India Company. Founded in 1602, the Company crushed the global markets through the peddling of textiles, spices, and other trivial items, at one point even dabbling in the trade of tulip bulbs. As the majority shareholder of the wildly successful VOC, Amsterdam thrived like it never had before.

A depiction of VOC ships

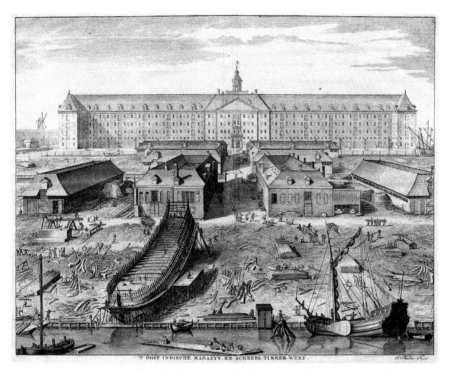

An 18th century depiction of the company's shipyard

The Company's shrewd marketing prowess and cutting business tactics empowered it to dominate international markets, but it was the VOC's fiscal savvy that allowed the Dutch to hold on to their recently acquired wealth. For one, the VOC created the first stock exchange the same year of its foundation, devised as a way to cover the expenses of their maritime endeavors. Nine years later, Dutch architect Hendrick de Keyser was commissioned to design and oversee the construction of the stock exchange's first headquarters. The headquarters at Rokin, named the "*Beurs van Hendrick de Keyser*" upon its completion, is regarded by many chroniclers as the oldest stock exchange venue in the world. The interior was sectioned off into four parts to cater to the 4 types of exchanges that transpired here – the classic stock exchange, the shippers' trade exchange, the corn exchange, and the commodity exchange. The *Amsterdamsche Wisselbank* (Bank of Amsterdam) was installed at the same time to streamline the activities and police the financial transactions between companies and individuals.

The dramatic population boom on Dutch soil further highlights the steadily growing prosperity of the locality at the time. In 1572, Amsterdam was populated by about 30,000, and just 50 years later, that number had soared to 105,000, many of them ambitious merchants hungry for a slice of that pie. It was amidst this atmosphere that the art of collecting slowly, but surely became cemented as a mainstream pursuit. Collecting, like the appreciation of tulips, was imported from outside of the continent. The royals and aristocracy of Ancient Egypt, Greece, and Rome are now believed to have been some of the earliest civilizations to engage in art-collecting. Some royals were so attached to their collections that they insisted upon being buried with them; case in point – King Tut, who was laid to rest with some of his favorite pieces from his collection, including a "luscious lapis lazuli encrusted gold-work." Roman emperors expanded their collections with the booty they swiped from their raids. Clusius himself was a keen collector, who often requested his sea-faring friends to bring home peculiar-looking fish and other eccentric man-made objects.

Naturally, as this trend became more prevalent, traditions and norms evolved. Collecting was no longer a cliquey hobby experienced by only the elites and their inner circles; even those in the lower classes began to partake, many of them supposedly owning a few paintings and small sculptures themselves. Enterprising businessmen leapt on the opportunity to capitalize on the trend, either by trading valuables with other parties to mutually satisfy one another's collections, or by establishing businesses dedicated to acquiring and selling art, manuscripts, seashells, and other trinkets and collectibles.

As the old saying goes, all things are better in moderation. While most played safely by this rule, amassing items at a pace that best suited them, some were such fanatical collectors that their feverish attempts at procuring the newest collectible inexorably led to their bankruptcies. The celebrated Dutch artist Rembrandt was one of those stricken by collection fever; an art collector himself with a special taste for Michelangelo originals, Rembrandt sunk so deep into debt that he was forced to auction off his house, and eventually his collection itself, to foot what he owed. On the other side of the spectrum, there was Emperor Rudolf II, whose *kunstkammer* was home to the following: "470 paintings, 69 bronze figures, 179 ivory objects, several thousand medals and coins, 403 Indian *curiosa*, 600 vessels of agate and crystal, 50 amber and coral pieces, 185 uncut diamonds and precious stones, 174 works of *faience*, 300 mathematical instruments, numerous taxidermies, and countless other items..."

On a similar note, the practice of speculation in the marketplace is a concept that was anything but alien to the Dutch. To better understand its roots, one must hark back to the creation of the world's first commodities, which arose out of crop production and the rearing of livestock. Following the agricultural revolution around 8500 BCE, neighboring tribes began to trade crops and livestock – commodities – with one another. Roughly 6,000 years later, Egyptian pharaohs seized control of the grain trade so as to regulate the stock and prices within the industry. By the time Ptolemy I took to the throne in the 4th century BCE, "all [grain] prices were fixed by fiat." *The Code of Hammurabi,* engraved upon Babylonian tablets, illustrated the set wages for services and labor that was to be shelled out annually "in per annum amounts of grain."

Ancient Greek authorities later published a set of decrees designed to safeguard and boost the local economies. The city of Athens, for example, banned exports, set fixed duties on imports, and issued laws against supply-tampering and other acts that manipulated the prices of grain and other commodities. Authorities took these decrees seriously, so much so that a band of Athenian grain merchants declared guilty of "hoarding and collusion" were put to death for their crimes.

The Dutch also modeled their 17th century economical practices on those of the resourceful 13th century Venetians. The *Ligatio pecuniae,* proclaimed in 1262, popularized the concept of coughing up an additional 5% interest to money lenders. The developments that followed in the fledgling credit market were explained by William N. Goetzmann, author of *The Origins of Value: The Financial Innovations that Created Modern Capital Markets,* who noted that "government credits were traded in a secondary market and financial derivatives, such as overdue interest – became diffused objects of trade."

When governmental control of individual industries began to slacken, suppliers and dealers alike were awarded more freedom to control the prices of their own products. Farmers and producers of other biodegradable goods factored in weather conditions, supply and demand, economical slumps, and even political events into their pricing. Moreover, as grain stock skyrocketed over the years, farmers and merchants had to find ways to profit while their product sat in storage. This, in turn, led to the creation of "futures agreements."

In 1531, Antwerp unveiled a building devoted to overseeing these financial and commercial transactions, and credit and risk became crucial components of this speculative business practice. Holy Roman Emperor Charles V of Hapsburg and his court seemed to have calculated the perils of precarious futures agreements, for they issued certain laws, including the requirement of valid contracts later that decade. These contracts, known as "forward contracts," or simply "forwards," were essentially documents allowing the purchaser of the product to acquire said product in the future at a price agreed upon during the signing of the contract. Later, merchants in Amsterdam instituted stellages, defined by Ann Berg, author of *The Rise of Commodity Speculation: From Villainous to Venerable,* as "forward contract[s] with an option by the buyer to annul the contract for a paid premium."

The mechanics of 17th-century futures and forward agreements were rather straightforward. Futures were "standardized," whereas forwards were typically negotiated behind closed doors. For example, if the price of grain was 10 guilders a bundle in 1630, a speculator, taking into account all the aforementioned risk factors, could choose to lock in the price by drawing up a futures agreement with his supplier. If the speculator anticipated an upcoming storm, for instance, they might choose to enter the agreement at once to avoid an inevitable spike in prices. As transformative as this new practice was, skeptics on the sidelines found it problematic, for it was never a win-win situation. If the storm did strike, crippling the farmer's supply the following year, the farmer would be forced to shoulder the often debilitating loss, whereas if prices continued to plummet, speculators – many of them bright-eyed, but inexperienced – took a hit.

Following a particularly pitiful harvest in 1556, which annihilated hordes of farmers bound by futures contracts – not to mention the thousands unable to afford basic foodstuff – Amsterdam's sheriff condemned the practice and accused the Flemish and German merchants manipulating the market of committing a "great evil." That year – then again in 1565 and 1571 – the local government issued a ban on forwards regarding "the manipulation of the trade in staple foods such as grain, fearing the social unrest which might follow price increases." And though a general disdain for speculation – which they termed *"windhandel,"* or "trading in the wind," - arose amongst the masses, forward contracts continued to be cranked out by the dozens. Few could have seen coming the speculation fever that lurked around the corner, for the object of desire seemed no more than a trifling luxury.

Promising Springs

Gerard M.'s picture of tulip fields

"Snow is both sides of the same page

It covers the grave and the tulip." - Richard L. Ratliff

The flourishing economy and financial innovations of the Netherlands in the early years of the 17th century had opened up a door that had previously been boarded up to the masses. For the first time, even fishermen, coopers, blacksmiths, and other unglamorous laborers dared to dream. No longer would their lowly societal rankings dictate their futures – anyone could make it big, it seemed, so long as they had money.

That being said, though many in the lower classes were being fed with rumors about their neighbors suddenly striking it rich seemingly overnight, the chances of happening upon such fortunes were slim to none. The average salary of skilled, but overabundant artisans at the time was about 300-500 guilders a year. If they remained frugal year-round, purchasing only what they absolutely needed, they might have been able to set aside anywhere between 20-50 guilders a year, equivalent to about one to two pounds of rye. Even if they managed to save up enough for a share in a relatively successful company, this was just one negligible share compared to the thousands of shares owned by affluent stockholders.

Given such circumstances, it is easy to see why these tulip schemes attracted the small-fry merchants, tempting many to not only invest heavily in tulips, but to become *bloemisten* (tulip growers and sellers) themselves. Those unfamiliar with the tulip business – or business in general – were most eager (or as some would say, most vulnerable) to dive into the ever-evolving tulip market.

On the face of it, the tulip business seemed simple enough, because the soaring demand, coupled with the extremely limited supply of tulips at the time, did wonders for their market value. Thus, tulip pushers could therefore charge as much as they saw fit, and though tulips were slow growers, aspiring tulip peddlers were certain that they would more than pay off. Patience was key, since tulips are plants and caring for them would be no more difficult than any other crop on the market

The accessibility of tulip startups to the masses was yet another one of the seemingly endless incentives. The land required to harvest these colorful spring beauties was minimal, so even a plot of land measuring no more than half an acre would do. Those who sported the greenest thumbs reportedly reaped plenty of tulips from nothing more than just a couple of pots.

The safest bet would be to dip into one's savings, but few, if any, could afford to do so. As such, the popularization of loans and mortgages made it easier to ensnare landless hopefuls. Some sought out loans or promised landowners a percentage of their future profits, while others mortgaged their tools, furniture, and even their homes to pay for the square of land they required. In hindsight, this was quite the gamble to say the least, but to these hopefuls, it was anything but, for they were positive they would be able to pay back their loans in full, including interest, by the following spring.

Tulips were fast gaining traction, a reality that was not lost on the underbelly of society. Eventually, criminals were also itching to profit from the fast-growing trade. Most crept into tulip gardens late into the evening and prised as many tulips as they could from the earth. Tulip thieves were apparently at one point such a pest that tulip farmers began to employ guards to patrol their gardens throughout the night.

Then, there were the *rhizotomi*, a derivative of a Greek word that translates into "root cutter." The *rhizotomi* spent their days scouring the countryside for rare tulips and bulbs, which they then sold to farmers, dealers, and collectors alike for a hefty price. While the act of obtaining tulips from the wild was perfectly legal, a considerable portion of unscrupulous root cutters tainted the reputation of the *rhizotomi*. Some of these dishonest, but crafty entrepreneurs replaced the rare bulbs with the seeds of common tulips, while others hired thugs to retrieve the sold bulbs from their customers. And since it was impossible to ascertain the appearance of the flower by simply assessing the bulb, some exaggerated their worth, while others fabricated backstories of nonexistent tulips entirely. The duped customers eventually wised up to these scams, but by then, it would be too late, for these "grifters" would have been several towns over, rendering them untraceable.

Be that as it may, it is now believed that the better part of those engaged were reputable, though somewhat naive businessmen. Many of the most trustworthy growers were based in Haarlem, who grew their product on the sandy, nutrient-rich soil outside the city limits.

Tulip painting was another unlikely profession that arose with the trend. As primitive as advertising was in those days, it was inherently fundamental in an increasingly competitive market. Like any other 17th century business, tulip dealers relied on word-of-mouth tactics and overly wordy fliers to make a name for themselves. To keep their voices from being drowned out by the growing crowd, tulip sellers enlisted the assistance of artists that specialized in still-life and botanical paintings. These artists were commissioned to produce paintings of tulips available for sale, which were then compiled into books; the visual imagery provided by browsing through these catalogs was more often than not, the final nudge needed for a sale.

These tulip albums, some of which contained up to over 100 unique pages, were works of art in more than just the literal sense of the phrase. Captured in either traditional watercolor or gouache (muted, or "opaque" watercolors), each page featured a lovely, exquisitely detailed image of a single tulip, sometimes garnished by a nice patterned vase, a striking insect cradled in one of its leaves, or smaller pictures depicting the stages of the tulip's growth. The type of tulip pictured was often scrawled onto the side or bottom of the page, along with the itemized number, name of the artist, and the date of the illustration's completion. Starkly missing on most of these albums were the prices of these tulips, for this allowed them to set whatever price best suited them at the time.

A 17th century watercolor of the *Semper Augustus*, the most expensive tulip sold

Contrary to what one might assume, the freelance painters hired to produce these albums were meagerly compensated for their stunning work, and the fact that these paintings were irreplaceable and difficult to duplicate seemed irrelevant. The creativity cultivated by the Dutch Renaissance was certainly as astounding as it was game-changing, but the congested field often left even the most talented artists with no choice but to accept peanuts, lest they be out of work. Jacob Isaaczoon van Swanenburg, the mentor of none other than Rembrandt, was subjected to this injustice; rather than receive money, Swanenburg was promised a loaf of bread for each tulip painting he produced. In a twist that would make these artists spin in their graves, these very same tulip books (of which only 20 or so exist in mint condition) are now worth about $20 million each.

The tulip album of Haarlem-based florist Pieter Cos was one of the most remarkable of its kind. This 54 page manuscript featured 33 gouache originals of tulips by Cos himself, along with a dozen more from Pieter Schagen and Pieter Holsteijn the Younger; the remaining 9 pages were watercolor illustrations of carnations and other exotic flowers.

An *Admiral van der Eijck* tulip, advertised in this Cos manuscript, sold for 1045 guilders on February 5, 1637

Like most other tulip albums, the illustrations in Cos' book were accompanied by the names of the tulip and its artist. What wasn't so orthodox was Cos' resolved inclusion of the flowers' weights, and even their prices. What's more, in place of names for some of these tulips were riddles, drawings, or rebuses, which were "punny" puzzles consisting of picture combinations and individual letters that spelled out or alluded to the name of the tulip. The slightly varying weights of these tulips were documented in "aasen" (1 aas = 0.048 grams; bulbs were usually sold per 500 or 1,000 aasen), and the price of every account sold provided in guilders. Of the 17 ultra-premium tulips pictured in Cos' album, the *Viseroij* (Viceroy) was listed as the cream of the crop. According to the inscriptions, the *Viseroij* bulbs were only sold twice at the prices of 3,000 and 4,200 guilders, roughly "15 or 20 times the annual salary of a schooled craftsman."

Another notable tulip album is the Judith Jan Leyster Book, now on display in Haarlem's Frans Hals Museum. As suggested by the title of the album, the paintings were created by Judith, among the few females who could call art their bread and butter, and one of the only two women to bear the title of "master" in the Haarlem Guild of St. Luke. Two of the *"Rozen"* tulips depicted in Judith's book have been made her namesake, one of which can be described as a fluffy tulip with a cream base, enlivened by feathery, apple-red streaks. The second tulip, which averages between 20 and 22 inches in height, is tinged with either a pastel peach or soft, "carmine-pink." As dictated by custom, Judith signed her illustrations – a capital "J" and a six-pointed asterisk, a clever play on her surname, meaning "lode star" in Dutch.

Judith Jan Leyster's *Blompotje (Flowers in u Vuse)* **(1654)**

Tricks of the Trade

"The tulip next appeared, all over gay,

But wanton, full of pride, and full of play;

The world can't show a dye but here has place;

Nay, by new mixtures, she can change her face..." - Abraham Cowley

As the demand for tulips continued to climb, tulip traders began to search for venues that would allow them to conduct their business freely. Most historians have come to assume that the lightweight purses of the tulip merchants had much to do with their inability to erect or consecutively pay rent for an exchange building of their own. Other chroniclers who saw the tulip as more of a rich man's sport, on the other hand, claim that they were rejected by all churches and most all public spaces, for these establishments vocally disapproved of the barely disguised speculative practices.

Why these moneyed men chose not to pool their money together for what was apparently a shoo-in is unclear, but whatever the case, most tulip farmers gathered in the only places that would have them: taverns, or as they were sometimes referred to, "colleges." The *Toelast,* a tavern-inn in the Grote Market of Haarlem, was one of the establishments most frequented by tulip traders. Other inns that bustled with tulip-related activity included *De Vergulden Kettingh* (The Golden Necklace), *Van de Sijde Specxs* (The Flitch of Bacon), all in Haarlem, as well as *De Mennoniste Bruyloft* (The Mennonite Wedding) in Amsterdam. Private tulip exchanges were just as common; most of these low-key transactions took place in the homes of tulip traders, but those who sought an added sense of security could request to meet in front of a notary, or on other neutral grounds.

It was here in these often cramped and dingy taverns, the poor lighting made even more dim by a permanent fog of tobacco smoke, that most tulip exchanges occurred. The prospect of unthinkable riches filled these traders with giddy excitement, and their high spirits were only further improved by their generous consumption of precisely that. Each time tulip traders clinched a deal, those selling the tulips paid a small premium to the middlemen, or facilitators of the deal. The commission – which tulip traders called *"wijnkoopsgeld,"* or "wine money" – paid to them was then used to purchase a round of ale or tobacco, and at times, even sessions with prostitutes. The *wijnkoopsgeld* varied depending on the prices and terms of the deal struck, but even when deals fell through, sellers were still made to fork over a small fee. Not only did this fee pay for the time of the mediator, it also doubled the seller's efforts when it came to brokering a deal.

The so-called "wine money" was only one facet to the full-bodied culture that developed within the tulip trading community. Like many fraternities, newcomers were subjected to hazing. Fresh faces, for one, were almost always singled out by veteran traders at the start of auctions and meetings, and called an assortment of derogatory names and epithets, usually "the new whore in our brothel."

Tulip traders were expected to abide by protocol, which seasoned traders knew inside and out. To begin with, novices could expect to be spurned if they were to bluntly request for a trade with no prior warning. Instead, tulip trading etiquette called for one to drop thinly veiled hints. A typical opener sounded something like this: "I have more than enough reds in my collection, but I should be so lucky to come across some of those darling yellows." When the other traders eventually cottoned on, both parties – the purchaser and the seller – entered one of two types of exchanges. A "secretary" was also appointed to record all the transactions.

The first of these exchanges was what the traders called "with the boards," a procedure usually requested by the potential buyer. Wood-framed slates and pillars of chalk were then distributed to the buyer and the seller. Buyers kicked off the exchange by scrawling down a price they were prepared to accept on their slate. Normally, experienced buyers inscribed a price they knew would be considered well below the market value of the tulip in question. Next, the seller jotted down his own price on his slate. If the seller was well-versed with the tricks of the trade, he wrote down a price that he knew surpassed the tulip's worth. Finally, the mediator, seated between them, collected both their slates, analyzed their prices, and determined the median. Either party could choose to renegotiate if they so wished, but an exchange would not be complete without the consent of both the buyer and the seller.

Traders who were looking to unload excess stock or fishing for new customers opted for the *in het ootje,* which directly translates into "in the little 'O.'" This was an auction of sorts, one that was conducted by tavern secretaries. Similarly, the prospective bidders were handed slates and chalk, only their boards came with a pre-drawn symbol: an "S" stacked on top of an "O," with a vertical line slashing down the center of both letters. On the bottom half of the "O," bidders were expected to scribble down the amount in stuivers (20 stuivers = 1 guilder) they wished to part with in terms of commission. The donation varied, but most chipped in about 2 to 6 stuivers, which was equivalent to about one or two rounds of drinks. The upper half of the "O" was the amount bidders wished to dedicate to the bulbs up for auction. The secretary, who served as the auctioneer, determined and announced the winning bid. To mark an auction complete, secretaries encircled and crossed out the symbol three times, the traders' version of "going, going, gone." Even so, the ball remained in the seller's court, for he could choose whether or not he wished to honor the price of the winning bid. If he chose not to, however, he was still made to dish out the *wijnkoopsgeld* written down on his slate.

Should the seller choose to honor the price at hand, the winning bidder handed over about a 5-10% deposit. The purchaser was then awarded either a notarized note or a contract promising him his batch of tulips when they blossomed the following spring, or whenever the arrangement was due. The remaining balance (the rest of the 90-95%) would also be settled on the date of the physical exchange.

This was the standard operating procedure, but some sellers were also known to engage in old-fashioned bartering, accepting valuable tools or goods as currency. One recorded instance (of many) indicates that a florist once managed to lock in his order with 4 cows as his deposit, and he later paid the rest of what was owed in cash the day he was delivered his sack of bulbs, which weighed no more than a quarter of a pound.

Inevitably, as the floral fad progressed further down the timeline, these unambiguous, no-nonsense methods morphed into a chaotic free-for-all. With more and more participants attempting to squeeze into the crowded market each passing day, many found themselves stampeded over or barricaded from even entering. Historians cannot be certain who it was that ignited this practice, but at one point, a tulip enthusiast was desperate enough to approach a contract/note-holder and offer the original buyer more money than he had paid for the bulbs, to which the original buyer readily accepted. This one supplementary transaction immediately added to the overall value of the tulip.

What ensued is best summed up by Rory Brosnan from *That Dam Guide*: "Then another trader realized that he...could do the same with the second person to town the contract, and then a fourth realized they could lever the contract from the third trader with an even bigger bid. And so on, for a fifth, sixth, or seventh owner of the contract. This type of trading caught on quickly, and spontaneously a futures market in tulips had developed in the United Provinces..."

What made this futures market especially risky was the fact that even tulip connoisseurs had no way of knowing what they were betting on, or how much the variety was worth until these bulbs actually bloomed. Even more nail-biting were the acts of God and other potentially devastating factors they had little to no control over, such as floods or botanical diseases that could partially or entirely affect the growth of the bulbs. The seeming nail to the coffin was the duration they were made to wait for what wasn't even a sure thing – florists had to wait 7-12 years for the first blossom, and even then, they only remained in bloom for a week. And still, all things considered, it was a gamble that apparently tens, if not hundreds of thousands were willing to take.

There is no specific date or year that marks the official commencement of the Dutch tulip trade. Records show exchanges that date to as early as the first years of the 17th century, but *Tulpenmanie* (Tulip Mania) only begun in earnest towards the late 1620s or early 1630s. It was a seasonal business, as bulbs usually flooded the market between the months of June and September.

In the early years of tulip trading, these flowers were sold by the bulb, but as the locals' obsession with tulips intensified, the more common, the value of mono-colored breeds, though still in high demand, steadily plummeted. Thus, as the trend inched closer to its climax, tulip dealers began to sell common breeds by the bed. The rarest breeds were then sold by the bulb, but dissent within the community soon led to the creation of a new unit of measurement.

The notion of sinking one's life savings into a single bulb with no tangible guarantees of success was, understandably, a risk that few were willing to venture. Bulbs differed in size as well, so even if one managed to procure the plumpest of bulbs, he or she could still be doomed to an underwhelming harvest. To cushion the blow on both ends, tulip traders introduced the "ace," each equivalent to about 1/20th of a gram, meaning that the price of the tulip now hinged on the weight of its bulb. Unfortunately, owing to the lack of regulations on futures markets regarding non-staple products, prices of tulips were unique in each city, which only further stirred the pot of confusion.

Nearly 400 years later, it is difficult to identify exactly how much the more common tulips cost prior to the mid-1630s, but by then, it would have already been well-established as a status symbol. Records show that four beds of "mediocre" tulips were sold for 200 guilders in 1611, making a bed of tulips 50 guilders a pop, or roughly a quarter of a skilled laborer's yearly wages. It might have been tough, but it wasn't outside the realm of possibility for one with a moderate amount of savings to try his luck in the field.

Those who attempted to hop on the bandwagon in the following years, however, would be presented with far loftier hurdles, judging by the rate of the price hikes. By 1612, the prices for the same breed of tulips had been hiked up to a staggering 225 guilders a bed. This was because tulip bulbs were being passed around on an average of up to 10 times a day. As Anne Goldgar, Professor of Early Modern History at King's College, explains, "No one wanted the bulbs, only the profits – it was a phenomenon of pure greed."

An excerpt from the *Amsterdam Tulip Museum* shines an even brighter light on the subject: "The presence of speculators is common in major economic bubbles – they bring in something of a 'fake demand,' where every seller can find a buyer (often another speculator). This only increased the frenzy around the contracts."

It was in the spring of 1633 that the tulip craze abruptly transitioned into a new chapter. Tulip traders awoke to the community abuzz with the news that a brand-new inn in Haarlem had been sold for three unidentified, but presumably rare bulbs. These firm, multi-layered pre-tulip nuggets had become a type of currency themselves, and a few weeks later, a farmhouse in the coastal region of Frisia was swapped for a small package of bulbs. Tulip breeders had to get more creative to keep themselves from getting entangled, and thereby lost in the weeds of this cut-throat market.

At the bottom of this four-level pyramid were single-color tulips – the reds, whites, and yellows – known as "*couleren.*" The two levels above housed dual-toned tulips – the "*rosen,*" which featured primarily white petals brightened up by splashes of reds and pinks (e.g., the Judith Leyster tulip, among the 400 or so other varieties that existed by 1635), and the "*violetten,*" (70 or so varieties) which had white petals marbled with streaks of pastel to vibrant, boysenberry purples, respectively.

The *"bizarden"* tulips, which loomed over the rest, came in only 24 varieties, and were by far the most desired of all the tulips. Their petals came with a canary-yellow base, and were beautifully striped with "flames" of caramel-browns, royal-reds, and deep violets. Unbeknownst to the 17th century traders, the tulips they lusted after the most were infected by a "benign mosaic virus," the "Tulip Breaking Virus," to be exact. Carlos Torres-Viera of *Contagium* explained the 7,000-year-old disease in the following passage: "[TBV] causes a redistribution of epidermal anthocyanin pigments and their segregation in irregular stripes, bars, thick stripes, spots, or "flames." Between the lines and stretch marks appear pure white or yellow spots...Often this interruption of ["broken"] color is restricted to strokes in the margins and tips of the petals and sepals. Flowers of pink, red, and purple colors develop striking changes. Those with dark streaks develop even darker colors...The mosaic virus affects the bulb, but not the seeds. The resulting color variation will be random, only reproducible by growing a plant from a bulb or its secondary buds..."

Clusius was among the few who questioned the appearance of these flames on the tulips, which he concluded weakened the flower, but it was only in the 19th century that botanists understood its true implications and classified it as a "viral disease." Those that sported these patterns were proven to have shorter lifespans and lower rates of reproduction. Furthermore, once the last of these varieties withered, there was no way of replicating them, rendering them extinct. Tulip dealers in the 17th century were, of course, oblivious to this important factoid, but even those who suspected this were just as keen to get their hands on these disease-riddled tulips, for these were truly limited edition in every sense of the word.

The ultimate holy grail of tulips was an unparalleled beauty they called the *"Semper Augustus."* Physician and historian Nicolaes van Wassenaer was supposedly one of the first to come across this peerless flower in 1623 during a visit to the garden of Adriaen Pauw, a director of the Dutch East India Company and future Grand Pensionary of Holland. In Wassenaer's own words, the petite paradise teemed with "many different tulips; in the middle of them was a cabinet surrounded with mirrors which threw back the reflection of the flowers so elegantly that it seemed like a royal throne... [Nested in these tulips] was the *Semper Augustus...*The color is white, with carmine on a blue base, and with an unbroken flame right to the top. Never did a blommist [sic] see a more beautiful one than this: no tulip has ever been in greater esteem..."

Still Life with Flowers by Hans Bollongier (1639) showcases the *Semper Augustus* tulip

The year of its apparent discovery, a daring – or perhaps impulsive – tulip trader reportedly offered a whopping 12,000 guilders (which could buy a handsome house in Amsterdam and more) to a florist who claimed to have 10 *Semper Augustus* bulbs on hand. Much to his dismay, the florist grudgingly rebuffed him, for he accurately forecasted the future value of his bulbs. Around the same time, another florist was offered 12 acres of fertile land for just one of his *Semper Augustus* bulbs. Once again, the buyer was refused, and as it turned out, for good reason. Within a decade, by 1633, the price of a single bulb had soared to 5,500 guilders. By January of 1637, a single bulb was worth 10,000. This is even more stupefying when taking into account this passage from *Tulipomania: The Story of the World's Most Coveted Flower and the Extraordinary Passions It Aroused*, authored by Mike Dash: "[10,000 guilders] was enough to feed, clothe, and house a whole Dutch family for half a lifetime, or sufficient to purchase one of the grandest homes on the most fashionable canal in Amsterdam for cash, complete with a coach house and an 80-ft garden – and this at a time when homes in that city were as expensive as property anywhere in the world..."

At this point, tulips were no longer a mere symbol of prestige; they defined the buyer, and at times became entwined with his legacy. One prime example is documented by Rembrandt in *The Anatomy Lesson of Dr. Nicolaes Tulp*, published in 1632, which illustrates why the Dutch surgeon-turned-mayor of Amsterdam decided to change his name. Nicolaes, born Claes Pieterszoon, felt compelled to rebrand himself before entering the exciting, but often shallow world of politics, and thus, added a new prefix to his first name. He adopted "Tulp" to honor the tulip carved into the front of his family home, and tulips also became the centerpiece of his heraldic emblem. Moreover, it was clear that those who purchased their homes with nothing but tulip bulbs were extremely proud of the fact. When that inn was sold in Amsterdam in 1633, the new homeowners made certain to immortalize the event by etching three tulips onto the facade.

By 1635, the public's fascination with tulips had spiraled into an unhealthy fanaticism. Countless tulip breeders supposedly contemplated around the clock new ways to improve the probability of "breakage" in their tulips. Some held their bulbs briefly over a crackling fire. Some buried the bulbs in homemade concoctions composed of earth, sand, shells, and an ample helping of pigeon excrement. Some soaked their precious bulbs in tubs brimming with wine, urine, and other natural substances for weeks on end, hoping that in doing so, it would also influence the future color palette of the tulips. Few, if any at all, purposefully exposed their bulbs to factors that could actually trigger these breakages, such as greenflies, blackflies, and other minuscule aphids that fed on the sap of tulips, or kept them in close proximity to other diseased bulbs.

The startling stories that dribbled out of the United Provinces in droves only further showcased the bewildering extent of *Tulpenmanie*. The first is a story that echoes the tale told by Joris Rye in the 1560s. Sometime in the 1630s, a practiced collector received a parcel of tulip bulbs from the Levant – amongst multiple other consignments – delivered to him by an unnamed sailor. Grateful for the parcel's safe arrival, the collector whipped up for the sailor a delicious breakfast dish with red herring. Stunned by the collector's magnanimity, he took it upon himself to pocket one of the bulbs, and headed off to the docks to enjoy the view with his breakfast. It was, after all, only an onion – or so he thought, figuring the collector would never miss it. As the kleptomaniac sailor would soon find out, he could not have been more wrong, because within a matter of minutes, the collector was well-aware of its absence, for this was no ordinary tulip. Quite the opposite, it was the *Semper Augustus*, worth an eye-watering 6,000 guilders a bulb, which was more than enough to employ his entire fleet for two years.

The collector and his men just about turned his entire estate upside down before the sailor finally sprang to mind. When they finally tracked him down, the seething collector found the ignorant sailor perched upon a pile of ropes, casually picking at the remnants of the strange-tasting "onion" wedged between his teeth. The collector yelled, "Do you know what you've done, you fool? You have just sumptuously feasted the Prince of Orange and the whole court of the Stadtholder!" Notwithstanding the sailor's stammering apologies, the collector elected to press charges, which landed the sailor behind bars for several months. Some accounts claim he never saw the light of day again.

Another story concerned an English traveler and amateur horticulturist who appeared to have more than overstayed his welcome. One afternoon, a tulip bulb poking out from the earth in the garden of a Dutch noble caught the traveler's eye. Believing it to be no more than an old plant that was past its prime, the traveler invited himself into the garden. He then knelt down next to the root, and retrieving the small blade in his boot, he begun to shave off the skin of the bulb. Right as he was about to inspect his work up close, a pair of hands seized him by the collar and hoisted him up to his feet.

"What in God's name are you doing?" the Dutchman purportedly demanded.

"Why, I'm peeling a most extraordinary onion, of course," came the traveler's sheepish reply.

"This is no onion, you twit – this is an Admiral Van der Eyck!"

"Thank you," said the traveler as he turned to a fresh page in his journal, clearly unaware of the gravity of his crime. "Are these admirals common in your country?"

"Death and the devil!" snarled the Dutchman before even a droplet of ink could bleed into the page of the traveler's journal. "Come before the syndic, and you shall see!"

Less than 20 minutes later, the guilty traveler was marched through the streets, his head hung in baffled shame as an angry mob followed in tow. Only upon his trial before the magistrate did the traveler learn that the onion root he had so recklessly peeled was really the bulb of a rare tulip, one worth 4,000 guilders. The foreign traveler was then imprisoned until he worked off the standing balance.

All that Glitters is Not Gold

"...The tulips should be behind bars like dangerous animals;

They are opening like the mouth of some great African cat..." - Sylvia Plath, "Tulips"

By 1636, the outbreak of tulip fever had become a presence so ubiquitous throughout the United Provinces – in particular, Haarlem, Rotterdam, Alkmar, Hoorn, and other towns – that the flower was being traded on the Amsterdam Stock Exchange. A substantial number of traders from nearby regions, such as in Paris and London, allegedly envious of the tulip traders' triumphs in the Netherlands, also began to show interest. The traders in England seemed especially committed to rousing the interests of local buyers, because tulips were, for a time, also traded on the London Stock Exchange, but it was far from the sure bet it appeared to be on Dutch soil.

While most of the tulip traders were ecstatic about the continuous climb of tulip prices, there was a small, but growing sector of spectators and traders alike who sensed something was amiss. "Still Life With a Vase of Flowers and a Dead Frog," an emblematic piece painted by Jacob Marrel, a tulip pundit himself, was produced in 1634. Pictured in dull colors and drenched in shadows is a diverse, but visibly wilting bouquet. Towering over the rest of the flowers is a tall and "rigid" red-and-white *Admiral Coornhardt* tulip, but the red-and-gold variant to its right has lost its color and is tilting away from it, on the verge of falling out of the vase. The Easter eggs outside of the vase provide even deeper meaning; the skinny worm lingering on the edge of the table, for example, represented the impending "death and decomposition" of the tulip craze. The dead frog, sprawled out "belly-up" across the right-hand corner of the table, is a medieval symbol of greed. Last, but not least, is the pitiful cluster of gooseberries, which alludes to the following proverb: "The words of the elders are like the gooseberry; bitter at first, then sweet."

Critics, scarce as they may have been, were more candid about their concerns, and they openly advised their friends against investing in such a tempestuous and unpredictable market, but few heeded their warnings. As a result, the price of tulips, which had become the fourth most exported Dutch commodity by 1636 (after gin, herring, and cheese), continued to escalate. On the 31st of December, 1636, a pound of *Switsers* bulbs – a tulip with butterscotch-yellow petals mottled with vibrant reds – sold for 125 guilders. Just a little over a month later, the same tulips were sold for 1,500 guilders, a record 1,100% increase.

A 1637 pamphlet advertising tulips

At this point in time, those just looking to break into the tulip trade were advised to invest a minimum of 100,000 guilders, which secured them a supply of roughly 40 bulbs. According to a historical Dutch currency converter, 100,000 guilders were estimated to be worth about "335 years of wages for an unskilled worker, or $9.4 million in current prices." With a wholesale price of about 2,500 guilders each (about $21, 700 today), the value of a single bulb was akin to the collective value of the following items: "four lasts (11,025 pounds) of rye, two lasts (5,510 pounds) of wheat, two hogsheads (480 liters) of wine, four tuns [sic] (1,010 gallons) of beer, 4,000 pounds of butter, 1,000 pounds of cheese, eight fat hogs, four fat oxen, a dozen fat sheep, a lavish bed, a suit of clothes, and a silver chalice."

On February 5, 1637, what many now consider to be the most consequential tulip auction was held in a guildhall in Alkmaar. This auction was sponsored by the recently deceased Wouter Bartelmiesz Winkel, a master tulip trader and the owner of a tavern/college called the "*Oude*

Schutters-Doelen." By the spring of 1636, Wouter boasted one of the most diverse and ached after tulip collections in existence, which consisted of the following: "70 fine or superbly fine tulips, representing about 40 different varieties, together with a substantial quantity of pound goods totaling about 30,000 aces of lower-value bulbs." The stars of his collection included a *violetten* named "Admiral van Enkhuizen," five "Brabansons," two Viceroys, three *rosens* called the "Admiral van der Eijck,*"* a "Bruyn Purper (Brown and Purple)," and seven variants of the "Gouda."

It was Wouter's wife, Elizabet Harmans, who passed on first, leaving the young widower to juggle his businesses and raise their seven children on his own. Sadly, Wouter failed to hold down the fort much longer, for the 30-something father himself died from an unspecified illness in the winter of 1636. The entirety of Wouter's incomparable collection was thus put up for auction the following February, and all profits were to be awarded to his surviving children.

Fortunately for the Winkel orphans, the auction was a massive success, attended by hundreds of tulip traders from all corners of the country. His favorite blossom, the Admiral van Enkhuizen, was purchased for 5,200 guilders by the same buyer who splurged an extra 21,000 guilders on a medley of other tulips in the same collection. By the end of just this one auction, the facilitators had cleared out over 100 bulbs and raked in a little over 90,000 guilders. The orphans were set up for several lifetimes, for the proceeds were equivalent to approximately $7,062,852-$17,657,130 USD today.

The following evening, during another auction in Haarlem's *Menniste Bruyloft*, 31-year-old Andries de Busscher offered the fateful pound of Switser bulbs for sale. After a particularly fierce round of bidding, it was 29-year-old Joost van Cuyck, an Amsterdam native, who was left standing, having snatched up the bulbs for 1,100 guilders. Like most traditional transactions, Van Cuyck paid a small percentage of what was due up front and submitted to De Busscher a promissory note confirming his intentions to pay the rest of the balance upon delivery. In return, he requested from De Busscher a signed document stating that De Busscher had in fact pledged the bulbs to Van Cuyck and only Van Cuyck as a recourse, an act that he declared irreversible. Van Cuyck's reasoning for this was the increasing number of sellers – either approached by poachers or became regretful of the settled upon price after the fact – wriggling out of contracts with no repercussions.

Both parties seemed wholly content about the transaction for the remainder of the day, but by the next morning, Van Cuyck was beginning to exhibit the first signs of buyer's remorse. Joined by his brother-in-law, Alister van de Cruijs, De Busscher approached Van Cuyck and proposed to him that Alister act as a "guarantor" or bodyguard, to put it crudely, for the delivery of the bulbs. To De Busscher's disappointment, a pale-faced Van Cuyck shook his head and replied, "I am not content with the guarantor. I wish to find [one] of my own liking." Alister assured Van

Cuyck of his expertise in the task at hand, and he even sweetened the deal by offering a glittering insurance fee of 1,200 guilders, but the buyer still refused to budge.

A number of witnesses later called upon testified in De Busscher's defense. One such witness, a tulip trader by the name of Johannes van Westrenen, insisted that he had personally shaken the hand of Van Cuyck to congratulate him on his purchase. Others backed Van Westrenen's statements, and added that they had seen him produce the customary wine money attached to the sale, along with an additional 2 shillings as alms for the poor.

Historians still don't know why Van Cuyck was so set on detaching himself from the deal. Some theorize that Van Cuyck was visited by a relative or close friend the same evening the sale was finalized, and that they frightened him out of the deal with worrying revelations, such as a report of the auction that took place in Haarlem on the 3rd of February, just three days prior. That event appeared to have been doomed from the beginning, for when the auctioneer disclosed the first lot of relatively rare tulips for sale, starting off the batch at 1,250 guilders, he was met with cricket-chirping silence. With a crack in his voice, the auctioneer subtracted 100 guilders from the starting price, and when he was again greeted by silence, he subtracted another 100, then another 100, until he had no choice but to remove the lot from the dock. This awkward dance was repeated for every last one of the lots on the agenda, and in the end, not one tulip was sold. As D. Hurst from the *History Channel* put it, "In less than 6 weeks, tulip prices nosedived more than 90%, from a high of some $76,000 to less than $1." This was the day, according to most chroniclers, that the tulip bubble finally burst.

This horror story was followed by reports of the 90,000 guilders apparently sold on the 5th at Alkmaar, which further served as evidence of a hopelessly turbulent, dead-end market. On the afternoon of February 7th, the day of Alister and De Busscher's proposal, tulip traders and florists in Utrecht began to assemble a cortege of delegates for an emergency conference that was to be held in Amsterdam, wherein they would brainstorm ways to counteract the crash. With this flood of revelations swirling around in Van Cuyck's head, it was no wonder he scrambled to pull out as urgently as he did.

What finally caused the bubble to burst? Author Rory Brosnan wrote, "Quite simply, the starting price of tulips had risen so grotesquely that nobody who wanted the tulips for themselves...was bidding. It was purely speculators, and they had unknowingly reached the tipping point where bidders no longer felt they could make money. They simply stopped bidding, and the market collapsed."

Naturally, those still embroiled in outstanding contracts following the crash were traumatized and maddeningly livid about their potential losses, to say the least. Those who had purchased fresh contracts were the most furious of them all, because they still owed the remaining balance and now had no chance of pawning off the suddenly worthless bulbs that would be delivered to them in the spring.

This started a kind of domino effect. Day after day, dozens of tulip traders defaulted, and nobles who had no concept of poverty were suddenly thrust into the pits of it, whereas many of the merchants who worked so hard to clamber out of it were reintroduced to it. Brotherly trust was now a value that had been flushed down the drains, with many accusing their families, friends, and neighbors of preying on them and seducing them into such a corrupt scheme. Further stifling the morale were the quickly circulating rumors about bankrupt traders tossing themselves into rivers and canals. Breeders who could not swallow the fact that they had previously let slip rare tulips for such a low price also reached the depths of depression. One such breeder, who was mourning the losses incurred from a "black" tulip, slit his own throat. Stories about permanent mental breakdowns were also common across the region.

With the government hesitant to interfere, authorities involved in the crumbling tulip communities dispatched their local deputies to Amsterdam, where they conducted another series of emergency meetings in an attempt to tackle the crash. Perhaps due to the absence of governmental guidance, not to mention the unimaginable agitation felt by those involved, these meetings were described by witnesses as being of "a stormy character." It was only on February 23, 1637 that the congregation decided that all contracts drawn up prior to the 30th of November, 1636 would be "declared null and void...and that, in those made after the date, purchasers should be freed from their engagements [by] paying 10% of [the outstanding balance] to the vendor." However, the tulip traders outside of the conference room would stand for no such agreement, giving rise to a surge of lawsuits revolving around breach of contract.

In April 1637, the Court of Holland stepped in at last and made the decision to temporarily suspend all outstanding contracts. To the untimely relief of the tulip community, the case made it before the Provincial Council at the Hague a few weeks later. There, officials mulled their options for weeks, but they could only come up with a plan that almost completely mirrored that of the deputies, for they could find no court in Holland that would dedicate themselves to the costly job of pursuing traders for payment. An excerpt from Charles McKay's *Extraordinary Popular Delusions and the Madness of Crowds* described the plan in detail: "Every vendor should, in the presence of witnesses, offer the tulips *in natura* to the purchaser for the sums agreed upon. If the latter refused to take them, they might be put up for sale by public auction, and the original contractor held responsible for the difference between the actual and the stipulated price."

Wagon of Fools **by Hendrik Gerritsz Pot (1637)**

This deadlock would not be lifted in full until January 1638, the year that individual cities began to establish proper committees dedicated to enforcing outstanding payments. Haarlem's *Commissarissen van de Bloemen Saecken* (Commissioners for Flower Affairs) was among the most active of the branches, convening twice a week, on Wednesdays and Saturdays. Floral contracts from there on out were no longer futures contracts, but rather "optional contracts." This meant that buyers could choose either to honor the contract in full, or to bow out by paying a fee of 3.5%.

If the losses they incurred from the crash weren't torturous enough, tulip traders became the butt of every joke. A wave of satirical songs, pamphlets, paintings, and even plays were produced about the foolish businessmen who fell prey to the deceptive charms of the *windhandel* again. "Satire on the Tulip Madness," painted by Jan Brueghel the Younger in 1640, is one particularly acerbic example. In this painting, traders are depicted as anthropomorphic apes. Some are haggling with others, armed with money satchels and open notebooks in hand, while others on the veranda gluttonously wolfed down a lavish feast. A pair of monkeys can also be seen hunched over a table draped in red velvet, obsessively counting their heaps of gold and silver. All the while, the tulips around them are discolored and withering, teetering on the brink of death.

The tulip bubble has since been juxtaposed with just about every crash that followed, including the South Sea Bubble, the Great Depression, Black Monday, the 2008 housing crisis, and others being referred to as "Tulip Mania 2.0." But while the veracity and extent of the madness in this period of time has gone mostly unchallenged by scholars for years, in large part thanks to the theatrical recounting in McKay's 1841 publication, a number of critics, the most prominent of them being Anne Goldgar, insist that the *Tulpenmanie* never reached the extremes often touted. According to Goldgar, "I always joke that [my book] should be called 'Tulipmania: More Boring Than You Thought. People are so interested in this incident because they think they can draw lessons from it. I don't think that's necessarily the case."

Goldgar and other skeptics assert that the merchant class was never wiped out, if only because the exorbitant price of entry made it an arena accessible to only closed clusters of the elite. One of the most salient points she presents that disputes this alleged myth is the fact that buyers never paid more than 2.5% as a deposit on average, and since many traders had already regarded the contracts as optional documents long before the government's intervention, they paid a comparably negligible nullification fee and were therefore freed from the bulk of the payments.

The second major myth is that the Dutch economy was so shaken by the crash that it took decades to recover. Skeptics argue that this price plummet was no more than a blip in the long run, pointing to the fact that the Dutch Golden Age lasted until about 1750. Furthermore, though tulips were indeed luxuries at one point, they were no more different than the villas, sports cars, jewelry, and other fancy toys purchased by the rich of today. Goldgar noted, "Far from bulbs being traded hundreds of times, I never found a chain of buyers longer than five, and most were far shorter. Far from every chimney sweep or weaver being involved in the trade, the numbers were relatively small, mainly from the merchant and skilled artisan class – and many of the buyers and sellers were connected to each other by family, religion, or neighborhood."

Simon Schama, author of *The Embarrassment of Riches: An Interpretation of Dutch Culture in the Golden Age*, blames radical Dutch Calvinists for propagating these distorted versions of the events. Schama noted, "The prodigious quality of [the Calvinist tulip traders'] success went to their heads, but it also made them a bit queasy...worried that the tulip-propelled consumerism boom would lead to societal decay."

The full truth in the now timeless tale of *Tulpenmanie* may never be verified, and its impact may never be properly gauged, but one thing is for sure: in the words of Robert Frost, nothing gold can stay.

Online Resources

Other Dutch history titles by Charles River Editors

Other titles about Tulip Mania on Amazon

Bibliography

Editors, R M. *1637 Tulip Mania*. 2017, www.rijksmuseum.nl/en/rijksstudio/timeline-dutch-history/1637-tulipmania. Accessed 8 June 2018.

Holodny, E. (2014, September 16). TULIPMANIA: How A Country Went Totally Nuts For Flower Bulbs. Retrieved June 8, 2018, from http://www.businessinsider.com/tulipmania-bubble-story-2014-9

Udell, C. (2013, April 10). 12 Fascinating Facts About Tulips. Retrieved June 8, 2018, from https://www.care2.com/greenliving/12-fascinating-facts-about-tulips.html

Editors, G. B. (2017). Interesting Facts on Tulips & Tulipmania. Retrieved June 8, 2018, from http://www.gardensbythebay.com.sg/content/dam/gbb/documents/media-room/2016/FOR WEBSITE-APPENDIX A Rediscover the Origins of the Tulip.pdf

Treybig, D. (2016, September 17). Tulip Mania. Retrieved June 8, 2018, from https://medium.com/five-guys-facts/tulip-mania-c904ba3c5692

Sooke, A. (2016, May 3). Tulip Mania: The Flowers That Cost More Than Houses. Retrieved June 8, 2018, from http://www.bbc.com/culture/story/20160419-tulip-mania-the-flowers-that-cost-more-than-houses

Goldgar, A. (2018, February 18). Tulip mania: The classic story of a Dutch financial bubble is mostly wrong. Retrieved June 8, 2018, from https://www.independent.co.uk/news/world/world-history/tulip-mania-the-classic-story-of-a-dutch-financial-bubble-is-mostly-wrong-a8209751.html

Editors, R. B. (2012, March 2). Bubbles: The Tulip Mania. Retrieved June 8, 2018, from http://readbubbles.blogspot.com/2012/03/fun-facts.html

Wood, C. (2008, December 11). The Dutch Tulip Bubble of 1637. Retrieved June 8, 2018, from https://www.damninteresting.com/retired/the-dutch-tulip-bubble-of-1637/

Editors, A. T. (2017, December 14). Why Did Tulips Lead To An Economic Bubble In 17th Century Holland? Retrieved June 8, 2018, from https://amsterdamtulipmuseumonline.com/blogs/tulip-facts/how-did-tulips-gain-their-speculative-prominence-during-tulip-mania

Carlson, T. (2017, April 10). WHAT WAS TULIP MANIA? Retrieved June 8, 2018, from https://www.1800flowers.com/blog/flower-facts/what-was-tulip-mania/

Beattie, A. (2016). Market Crashes: The Tulip and Bulb Craze (1630s). Retrieved June 8, 2018, from https://www.investopedia.com/features/crashes/crashes2.asp

Boissoneault, L. (2017, September 18). There Never Was a Real Tulip Fever. Retrieved June 8, 2018, from https://www.smithsonianmag.com/history/there-never-was-real-tulip-fever-180964915/

McKay, C. (2011). Extraordinary Popular Delusions And The Madness Of Crowds (M. J. Kosares, Ed.). Retrieved June 8, 2018, from http://www.usagold.com/gildedopinion/mackay-tulip-mania.html

Baluch, J. (2018, January 12). 25 SENSATIONAL QUOTES OF TULIPS. Retrieved June 8, 2018, from http://www.queentulip.com/2018/01/25-sensational-quotes-of-tulips.html

Shane, D. (2017, December 8). Bitcoin vs history's biggest bubbles: They never end well. Retrieved June 8, 2018, from http://money.cnn.com/2017/12/08/investing/bitcoin-tulip-mania-bubbles-burst/index.html

French, D. (2007, May 26). The Truth About Tulipmania. Retrieved June 11, 2018, from https://mises.org/library/truth-about-tulipmania

Planes, A. (2013, February 3). The Stupidest Bubble in History. Retrieved June 11, 2018, from https://www.fool.com/investing/general/2013/02/03/the-stupidest-bubble-in-history.aspx

Goldgar, A. (2007). Tulipmania: Money, Honor, and Knowledge in the Dutch Golden Age. Retrieved June 11, 2018, from http://press.uchicago.edu/Misc/Chicago/301259.html

Weber, M. J. (2018, January 10). That Time Tulips Crashed the Economy (Maybe). Retrieved June 11, 2018, from https://medium.com/@mjosefweber/that-time-tulips-crashed-the-economy-a3e00389ef87

French, D. (2018, March 29). Tulip Mania, Not a Myth. Retrieved June 11, 2018, from https://fee.org/articles/tulip-mania-not-a-myth/

Stallings, A. E. (2009, June). Tulips. Retrieved June 11, 2018, from https://www.poetryfoundation.org/poetrymagazine/poems/52602/tulips-56d23134329fa

Shinners, R. (2015, July 17). 19 Facts Every Tulip Lover Should Know. Retrieved June 11, 2018, from https://www.countryliving.com/gardening/a35956/tulip-fun-facts/

Editors, H. (2017). History of tulips in Holland. Retrieved June 11, 2018, from https://www.holland.com/global/tourism/discover-holland/traditional/tulips/history-of-tulips-in-holland.htm

Raven, S. (2014, October 25). The history of the tulip. Retrieved June 11, 2018, from https://www.sarahraven.com/articles/the_history_of_the_tulip.htm

Editors, N. W. (2015, December 21). Tulip. Retrieved June 11, 2018, from http://www.newworldencyclopedia.org/entry/Tulip

Editors, A. M. (2017, September 25). Origins Of The Word Tulip. Retrieved June 11, 2018, from https://amsterdamtulipmuseumonline.com/blogs/tulip-facts/origin-of-the-word-tulip

Bukey, E. (2018, March). The Flowery Journey of Tulips From the Ottoman Empire to Europe. Retrieved June 12, 2018, from http://mvslim.com/the-flowery-journey-of-tulips-from-the-ottoman-empire-to-europe/

Editors, N. (2016, February). Day of the Tulip. Retrieved June 12, 2018, from http://www.nordstjernan.com/news/sweden/6104/

Editors, H. B. (2017). THE TULIP'S EXOTIC ORIGINS. Retrieved June 12, 2018, from http://www.hortus-bulborum.nl/about-the-tulip/tulipmania

Ronson, A. (2017). TULIP MANIA. Retrieved June 12, 2018, from http://www.aronson.com/in-depth/tulip-mania/

Editors, D. L. (2016, November 21). Courting Catastrophe: Tulip Mania and Diamond Mania. Retrieved June 12, 2018, from https://www.thediamondloupe.com/articles/2016-11-21/courting-catastrophe-tulip-mania-and-diamond-mania

Editors, P. S. (2017, July 17). A Brief History of Tulips. Retrieved June 12, 2018, from https://blog.parkseed.com/2017/07/17/tulip-history/

Torres-Vierra, C. (2017, August 16). Tulips Went Viral: The First Speculative Bubble. Retrieved June 12, 2018, from http://www.contagium.org/tulips-went-viral-the-first-speculative-bubble/

Editors, E. B. (2018, March 29). Carolus Clusius. Retrieved June 12, 2018, from https://www.britannica.com/biography/Carolus-Clusius

Editors, R. (2018, April 24). Carolus Clusius. Retrieved June 12, 2018, from https://www.revolvy.com/main/index.php?s=Carolus Clusius

Editors, E. W. (2017). Carolus Clusius. Retrieved June 12, 2018, from http://botany.edwardworthlibrary.ie/herbals/seventeenth-century/carolus-clusius/

Editors, G. N. (2015). Carolus Clusius, the Leiden Botanical Garden, and the Tulip. Retrieved June 12, 2018, from http://geography.name/carolus-clusius-the-leiden-botanical-garden-and-the-tulip/

Stilo, A. (2009). Carolus Clusius (Charles de l'Ecluse). Retrieved June 12, 2018, from http://penelope.uchicago.edu/~grout/encyclopaedia_romana/aconite/clusius.html

Allen, R. (2017). History of Daffodils and Tulips. Retrieved June 12, 2018, from https://www.americanmeadows.com/history-daffodils-tulips

Editors, C. B. (2014, September). Clusius, tulips, and the first bubble. Retrieved June 12, 2018, from https://www.chicagobotanic.org/library/stories/clusius-part-2

Karabell, S. (2017, December 25). Lessons From The Dutch Golden Age: What Really Makes A Nation Great? Retrieved June 12, 2018, from https://www.forbes.com/sites/shelliekarabell/2017/12/25/lessons-from-the-dutch-golden-age-what-really-makes-a-nation-great/#5ea787467e28

Mendelssohn, J. (2017, November 15). Rembrandt, capitalism and great art: The Dutch golden age comes to Sydney. Retrieved June 12, 2018, from https://theconversation.com/rembrandt-capitalism-and-great-art-the-dutch-golden-age-comes-to-sydney-87429

Sussman, A. L. (2017, October 18). The Dutch Golden Age Gave Us Artists and Dealers as We Know Them Today. Retrieved June 12, 2018, from https://www.artsy.net/article/artsy-editorial-dutch-golden-age-artists-dealers-today

Editors, A. (2017). Amsterdam in the Dutch Golden Age: When money already made the Dutch world go round. Retrieved June 12, 2018, from https://www.amsterdo.com/amsterdam-in-the-dutch-golden-age-when-money-already-made-the-dutch-world-go-round/

Culotta, A. (2017, November 20). A Brief History of Art Collecting. Retrieved June 12, 2018, from https://artlandapp.com/a-brief-history-of-art-collecting/

Editors, V. A. (2017). Early Art Collectors. Retrieved June 12, 2018, from http://www.visual-arts-cork.com/art-collectors.htm#antiquity

Belisle, A. (2017). A BRIEF HISTORY OF COLLECTING. Retrieved June 12, 2018, from http://www.artuner.com/insight/brief-history-collecting/

Editors, B. B. (2008). History of the Dutch stock exchange. Retrieved June 12, 2018, from https://beursvanberlage.com/history-of-the-dutch-stock-exchange

Editors, U. C. (2016). Understanding the History of Commodities Markets and Futures Market. Retrieved June 12, 2018, from https://www.universalclass.com/articles/business/investments/understanding-the-history-of-commodities-markets-and-futures-market.htm

Berg, A. (2008, July 3). The rise of commodity speculation: From villainous to venerable. Retrieved June 12, 2018, from http://citeseerx.ist.psu.edu/viewdoc/download?doi=10.1.1.472.5383&rep=rep1&type=pdf

Thompson, E. A., & Treussard, J. (2002, December 31). Tulip Mania: Fact or Artifact? Retrieved June 12, 2018, from http://www.dklevine.com/archive/thompson-tulips.pdf

Stilo, A. (2017). Tulip Mania. Retrieved June 13, 2018, from http://penelope.uchicago.edu/~grout/encyclopaedia_romana/aconite/tulipomania.html

Brosnan, R. (2017, March). The Epic Story of the Dutch Tulip. Retrieved June 13, 2018, from https://thatdamguide.com/story-dutch-tulip/

Coogan, R. (2015, August 4). How much does tulips (flower) costs in your country? Retrieved June 13, 2018, from https://www.quora.com/How-much-does-tulips-flower-costs-in-your-country

Stilo, A. (2015). Conrad Gesner. Retrieved June 13, 2018, from
http://penelope.uchicago.edu/~grout/encyclopaedia_romana/aconite/gesner.html

Editors, I. (2017). Forward Contract. Retrieved June 13, 2018, from
https://www.investopedia.com/terms/f/forwardcontract.asp

Editors, I. (2017). Futures Contract. Retrieved June 13, 2018, from
https://www.investopedia.com/terms/f/futurescontract.asp

Editors, O. G. (2017). Difference between a Futures Contract and a Forward Contract.
Retrieved June 13, 2018, from http://www.theoptionsguide.com/difference-between-futures-and-forwards.aspx

Editors, E. (2013, October 4). Was tulipmania irrational? Retrieved June 13, 2018, from
https://www.economist.com/free-exchange/2013/10/04/was-tulipmania-irrational

Goldgar, A. (2018, April 17). Tulipmania: An Overblown Crisis? Retrieved June 13, 2018,
from https://www.historytoday.com/anne-goldgar/tulipmania-overblown-crisis

Editors, S. H. (2014, June 16). Tulip Mania: The First Big Bust. Retrieved June 13, 2018, from
https://searchinginhistory.blogspot.com/2014/06/tulip-mania-first-big-bust.html

Stilo, A. (2015). Semper Augustus. Retrieved June 13, 2018, from
http://penelope.uchicago.edu/~grout/encyclopaedia_romana/aconite/semperaugustus.html

Inglis-Arkell, E. (2012, April 27). The Virus that Destroyed the Dutch Economy. Retrieved
June 13, 2018, from https://io9.gizmodo.com/5905247/the-virus-that-destroyed-the-dutch-economy

Zweig, J. (2015, September 3). THE MUSEUM OF ART AND FINANCE, GALLERY 1:
TULIPMANIA. Retrieved June 13, 2018, from http://jasonzweig.com/the-museum-of-art-and-finance-gallery-1-tulipmania/

Van Osnabrugge, W. (2016). Money in the 17th century Netherlands. Retrieved June 13, 2018,
from http://vanosnabrugge.org/docs/dutchmoney.htm

Editors, I. I. (2017). Prices and wages and the cost of living in the western part of the
Netherlands, 1450-1800. Retrieved June 13, 2018, from http://www.iisg.nl/hpw/brenv.php

Juneja, P. (2016), Tulip Mania of the 17th Century. Retrieved June 13, 2018, from
https://www.managementstudyguide.com/tulip-mania-of-17th-century.htm

Editors, W. (2017). Tulip book of P. Cos. Retrieved June 13, 2018, from
https://www.wur.nl/en/Value-Creation-Cooperation/Facilities/Library/Special-
Collections/Books-journals/Tulip-book.htm

Editors, M. D. (2013, December 3). Judith Leyster and Tulip madness. Retrieved June 13,
2018, from https://mydailyartdisplay.wordpress.com/2013/12/03/judith-leyster-and-tulip-
madness/

Editors, G. (2018). Tulipa "Judith Leyster" (Triumph Tulip). Retrieved June 13, 2018, from
https://www.gardenia.net/plant/tulipa-judith-leyster-triumph-tulip

Editors, H. G. (2007, February 9). A Conversation for Handy Gardening Tips. Retrieved June
13, 2018, from https://h2g2.com/edited_entry/A328772/conversation/view/F40812/T3875313

Colombo, J. (2012, June 15). The Dutch "Tulip Mania" Bubble (aka "Tulipomania").
Retrieved June 13, 2018, from http://www.thebubblebubble.com/tulip-mania/

Editors, E. L. (2017). The Tulipomania. Retrieved June 13, 2018, from
http://www.econlib.org/library/Mackay/macEx.html?chapter_num=4#book-reader

Narron, J., & Skeie, D. (2013, September 22). Crisis Chronicles: Tulip Mania, 1633-37.
Retrieved June 13, 2018, from http://ritholtz.com/2013/09/crisis-chronicles-tulip-mania-1633-37/

Dash, M., PhD. (2010, September 27). Tulipomania. Retrieved June 13, 2018, from
https://www.slideshare.net/mikedash/tulipomania

Editors, M. A. (2011, September 13). Tulipmania! Retrieved June 13, 2018, from
http://maddiesancestorsearch.blogspot.com/2011/09/tulipmania.html

Laskow, S. (2016, April 28). The Most Beautiful Tulip in History Cost as Much as a House.
Retrieved June 13, 2018, from https://www.atlasobscura.com/articles/the-most-beautiful-tulip-in-
history-cost-as-much-as-a-house

Partington, R. (2017, December 2). Bitcoin bubble? The warnings from history. Retrieved June
13, 2018, from https://www.theguardian.com/business/2017/dec/02/bitcoin-bubble-the-warnings-
from-history

Sarudy, B. W. (2017, March 8). Economics in the Garden - 1600s great tulip folly - Tulip
mania! A speculative economic bubble... Retrieved June 13, 2018, from
https://bjws.blogspot.com/2017/03/economics-in-garden-1600s-great-tulip.html

Editors, E. N. (2017). The Orphans of Wouter Winkel. Retrieved June 13, 2018, from
https://erenow.com/modern/tulipomania-the-story-of-the-worlds-most-coveted-flower/13.html

Hurst, D. (2014, February 3). TULIPOMANIA COLLAPSES. Retrieved June 13, 2018, from https://www.historychannel.com.au/this-day-in-history/tulipomania-collapses/

Gross, D. (2004, July). Bulb Bubble Trouble. Retrieved June 13, 2018, from http://www.slate.com/articles/business/moneybox/2004/07/bulb_bubble_trouble.html

Dash, M. (2011). *Tulipomania: The Story of the World's Most Coveted Flower and the Extraordinary Passions it Aroused*. Hachette UK.

Bilginsoy, C. (2014). *A History of Financial Crises: Dreams and Follies of Expectations*. Routledge.

Free Books by Charles River Editors

We have brand new titles available for free most days of the week. To see which of our titles are currently free, click on this link.

Discounted Books by Charles River Editors

We have titles at a discount price of just 99 cents everyday. To see which of our titles are currently 99 cents, click on this link.

www.ingramcontent.com/pod-product-compliance
Lightning Source LLC
Chambersburg PA
CBHW062349240325
24027CB00032B/1060